# Your Dream Pet Cockatiel

*Twenty-first Century Care, Feeding, and Bonding*

by

Darla Birde

♫♫♫

**Discover one of the world's most beloved pet parrots...**

This complete twenty-first-century guide will give you everything you need to get started with your pet cockatiel, one of the world's most popular pet birds. Even if you're completely new to keeping a bird as a pet, this compact but complete book will give you the tools you need to develop a long-lasting relationship with your feathered companion.

D1736342

# Copyright &
# Legal Note

©2019 by Darla Birde & Dreambirbs Publishing
All rights reserved.

No portion of this book may be reproduced in any form without written permission from the author, except for brief (less than one sentence) quotes used for the purposes of review. Brief portions of this material were previously published in a different format.

I've made every effort to ensure that the information in this book was correct, but a book is never a substitute for your good judgment or the good judgment of an avian vet. If your bird is sick, don't wait. Contact an emergency vet for help right now. For the record, I *never* assume any liability to any reader for any loss, damage, or disruption caused by an error or an omission in this book, regardless of the cause of the error or omission, including accidents, negligence, or acts of God.

Please Note: It is a violation of international copyright law to post this book to free or sharing sites.

# Table of Contents

# How Cockatiels Stole Our Hearts

The cockatiel was once a rare and mysterious parrot unknown to the majority of the world's population. According to legend, one of these "little cockatoos" was among the prizes that the crew of the *HMS Endeavour* sailed off with in late 1770, after Captain James Cook and his crew completed the first of their voyages to find what they called Terra Australis Incognito.

Today, we call it Australia, the self-proclaimed "land down under," famous around the globe for its unique eco-system and personable parrot species. The cockatiel's native habitat in the dry interior of the Australian continent could be harsh. Like many other desert species, they evolved to be nomads, traveling in flocks to locate water sources. As a result, they are strong, slim, and aerodynamic, capable of flying for long distances on a relatively dry diet that includes an abundance of seeds from fire-resistant Australian acacia shrubs and trees.

Their natural traits soon brought them to the attention of wealthy European bird collectors. Although the natural 'tiel gives the overall impression of being a mid-sized gray bird, its jaunty crest, white wing patches, and orange cheeks caught the eye. Other parrots might have flashier feathers or learn to speak more words, but the cockatiel offered multiple advantages that made it a highly desirable pet or aviary bird.

*They were easy to feed. No complicated diets needed here. These birds naturally enjoy dry seed picked up from the ground.

*As hardy nomads, they were tolerant and resilient to change, instead of being touchy hothouse specimens.

*They proved eager to breed when food, water, and a safe nesting site was available. Wild cockatiels must hurry to nest whenever the rainfall comes, so these birds have evolved to breed efficiently in an abundant environment.

*Before the invention of DNA tests in the late twentieth century, most parrots were tough to sex. However, adult normal gray cockatiels have a clear difference between male and female, which made it easy for early bird breeders to set up successful pairs.

*Since they were a social species adapted to large flocks, they were bold and cheerful, capable of being real pets who enjoyed their people and other aviary birds.

With all these advantages, it doesn't really matter whether they sailed on the first voyage of the *Endeavour* or not. They were becoming better known, and there were multiple other voyages that delivered these personable parrots to Europe. At some point, they picked up their scientific description and Latin name, *Nymphicus hollandicus*. By the mid-1800s, they were being bred in France, Germany, and England.

As the nineteenth century progressed, Australia began to appreciate the value of its unique wildlife. They banned the export of native birds in 1894. Since it was such a reliable breeder in captivity, the cockatiel didn't miss a step in its spread across the rest of the world. By 1910, the first breeding pair of 'tiels had reached the United States.

As more and more breeders enjoyed success, they began to develop a fascinating selection of color mutations based on a palette of grays, silvers, pearls, whites, cinnamons, and yellows. The fun of discovering or developing a new color mutation encouraged even more people to enter the hobby. This once-rare species reserved only to a few wealthy Europeans became one of the world's most popular pet parrots.

Only the budgerigar and the peach-faced lovebird can rival its popularity.

The cockatiel continues to offer pet owners and hobby breeders the same advantages today:

*Easy to feed on widely available, inexpensive food. With a few updates to the old-fashioned diets, your cockatiel has a life expectancy of twenty years or even longer.

*Young birds are easy to tame and highly social. They love winning your attention, but they can also learn to go to others and to play happily with other cockatiels or even other pet birds.

*There is a strong hobby to support breeders who would like to learn to show prize birds and/or create beautiful mutations.

*While they are poor talkers, they do want to please you, and many of them can be trained to be fine whistlers who can learn human tunes.

# Before You Choose A Cockatiel

For its size, the cockatiel (like most other parrots) is a long-lived pet. A wild 'tiel in its harsh environment full of drought, fire, and feisty birds of prey can expect to live ten to fourteen years. Captive birds can live even longer, up to age twenty or even beyond. At the time of writing, the Guinness Book of World Records states that the oldest known cockatiel was Sunshine, first purchased in 1983 in Colorado and confirmed to be thirty-two years old on January 27,

2016. This author has heard unconfirmed rumors of even older birds.

You and your family will be spending a considerable percentage of your life with your new cockatiel, especially if you get your bird as a young fledgling. Therefore, you want to think carefully before you bring your new bird home. Is this really the right pet for you?

Consider the following issues.

## Does anyone in the home have asthma or allergies?

COCKATIELS DON'T JUST *look like* miniature cockatoos. They actually *are* true members of the cockatoo family. Indeed, they're the only cockatoo with a long slender tail to go with the crest instead of a shorter, stubbier tail.

Cockatoos are wonderful birds packed with personality, but they do come with one serious drawback— their dander, also known as "cockatoo dust."

This white powderlike substance may irritate some people. As the saying goes, ask your doctor.

And, yes, that does mean you'll spend extra time dusting and cleaning up after your cockatiel. I usually spritz my personal 'tiel with clear water or a special feather spray twice a week, but the dust still manages to escape into the wild.

If you don't have time for extra cleaning, or if you're annoyed about little dust particles somehow flying around two hours after you thought you just cleaned the place, the cockatiel may not be the right bird for you.

## Do you really want a talking bird?

COCKATIELS AREN'T THE most talented talkers going. Some birds do learn to say a few words, but this species is a poor choice for the person who has their heart set on a bird that speaks clearly and accurately in a human language. It would be unfair to choose a cockatiel only to rehome your bird later because it can't speak well.

However, if you are just as happy with a singing bird, maybe the cockatiel is the perfect choice. Even if they can't talk much, they can often learn to whistle human tunes with surprising verve.

For example, *The Andy Griffith Show* has been off the air for decades, but it lives on because it has become traditional to teach talented cockatiels to whistle the opening theme song. For whatever reason, this tune seems to captivate the cockatiel imagination. You can find the original theme song, as well as plenty of cockatiels performing it, on a quick search of YouTube.

In reality, any song that can be whistled is a prime candidate for teaching your cockatiel. For instance, a cockatiel whistling, "If You're Happy and You Know it," has received over eight million views on YouTube. If you start early and work patiently with your bird, who knows? You too could produce an internet sensation.

# Do you have enough time to spend

# with your bird?

COCKATIELS ARE SOCIAL birds. They are not pretty flowers who live to make a fine show in a cage. They expect to come out, maybe sit on your hand or shoulder, and get involved in the family's activities. They won't be happy if they are left alone in a silent house for long hours of the day.

If you are busy and extremely pressed for time, a cockatiel might not be your best choice. Instead, consider a pair of finches, canaries, or lovebirds. These birds are easy to care for and relatively low maintenance, and they are happy to live out their lives by focusing on their friend or partner in their shared flight or aviary.

Cockatiels evolved in the hustle and bustle of a large nomadic flock. A solo bird, kept apart from friends and family, will become depressed and may not live out its normal lifespan. A silent house doesn't seem natural to the 'tiel.

You should adopt a new cockatiel at a time in your life when you are confident of being able to spend time with your bird. Not just "quality" time, but casual, hanging out, listening to music or watching television, time. Your pet enjoys being with you on your shoulder or hand, even if you're not doing anything all that exciting. Being close to you can mean the world to your 'tiel.

## Do you already have other pets?

PEOPLE WHO OWN CATS, ferrets, or dog breeds developed to capture birds should almost never own cockatiels. We've all seen those oh-so-cute Instagram photographs of a curious cockatiel playing with somebody's cat or dog. Just... don't. The chance of disaster is huge. Cockatiels are friendly, social, and trusting. On top of that, they possess a natural instinct to fly to the ground from time to time to seek out seeding grasses.

Cats, ferrets, and a few dog breeds have their own natural instinct to seize and maybe kill prey on the ground that looks like easy pickings. If that instinct is triggered, they may not be able to resist the compulsion. It isn't fair to put them in a situation where they are expected to resist temptation.

I've known people who lost their cockatiels to their cats, and they blame themselves for years.

Don't bring a new bird into a high-risk situation. If you already own a cat, ferret, or a dog breed developed to chase birds or small prey, you are not really able to provide your cockatiel with a safe, appropriate home. The time is simply not right for cockatiel ownership.

That said, the social cockatiel doesn't ask to be your only pet, and they can be a fine addition to a home even if you already own other birds. Most of the time, you'll want to offer your 'tiel its own cage and sleeping quarters, but I've kept them safely in aviaries with a multiple of species, and you can learn to do the same with the right care.

And it is very common for pet cockatiels to happily share birdie play-gyms under supervision with a surprising variety of small or mid-sized parrots. This kind of supervised play can be a lot of fun and excellent for your little flock's mental and physical health.

Cockatiels can share space. They just shouldn't be asked to share that space with a potential predator.

## Are you very sensitive to noise?

WHILE I WOULDN'T CONSIDER cockatiels the noisiest birds around, some of them— especially a non-singing adult female— can have a rather loud, annoying call when they're trying to get your attention. The calling might become obnoxious if you go through a busy period in your life when the cockatiel feels you're not spending enough time and attention on the bird.

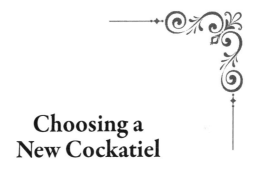

# Choosing a
# New Cockatiel

Although breeders today work with a larger number of parrot species, the cockatiel remains one of the most popular pet choices around. In many areas, it has become less common for pet stores or breeders to allow walk-in traffic. That isn't a bad thing. Closed aviaries can help protect the health of baby birds, and pet supply stores that don't sell birds cut down on the number of impulse purchases. However, it does mean that you will have to dig around a little to locate the best cockatiel resources in your communities. There are good babies out there. You just have to find them.

*(Note: If you already know you're getting an older bird, you can skip ahead to the chapter on adopting older birds.)*

Ask around. Network. There's nothing wrong with exploring dedicated Facebook groups and bird clubs, as long as you're good at rising above interpersonal drama. Some people enter various groups and then pound the drum for arguments that divide the community. I would rather avoid people who want to pit breeders against rescues. There's a place for responsible breeders, and there's a place for rescue. Take your time to make the right decision for you.

If your intuition tells you there's something wrong, listen. There will always be another opportunity to locate your perfect cockatiel. One of my personal rules is to avoid dealing with anyone who engages in online drama. Research everybody. And trust your gut.

You should also ask about any health guarantees. Some breeders may offer you a short period of time to get your new bird checked out by an independent vet.

This author believes no beginner should ever buy sick or injured birds. Please make every effort to buy a strong, healthy bird from a responsible operation.

Of course, everybody starts out planning to buy a healthy bird. However, the con artists in the community have developed every trick in the book for playing on the soft hearts of bird lovers. If you become aware of an abusive situation, report it to the local authorities. Don't try to fix it yourself by buying the birds.

Every bird you buy from an abuser represents cash money that encourages the abuser to keep doing their thing. Don't give unethical people a financial incentive to remain in the bird breeding business. You want to reward ethical breeders who truly care about their birds.

Most cockatiel breeders hand-feed their babies to create the best possible pets. You won't need to tame your new baby because the youngster will arrive already knowing that humans are part of their flock. Some breeders may allow you to visit your baby during the weaning process. They may even sell you the bird or allow you to put a deposit on your baby.

However, a responsible breeder will never, ever send an inexperienced person home with an unweaned baby. You must be able to prove your ability and past experience to wean the bird.

Here again is an area where a con artist might play on your love for birds. The slob breeder who doesn't feel like going through the entire weaning process may weave a compelling story about how you, the newbie cockatiel owner, can develop a richer bond by weaning the bird yourself. Actually, they just want to cut their hours and get to the money.

Hand-weaning a baby cockatiel is a skill developed with lots of practice with the help of a more experienced hand-feeder. It isn't something you can do perfectly on your own at home in your spare time. Most people who pick up this book don't have the experience to hit all the marks you need to hit to safely wean a baby bird.

Check this step-by-step list of items you'd need to know:

*How to sterilize and set-up the cockatiel brooder.

*Safe temperature, humidity, and lighting combination needed to prevent the growth of bacteria and to promote the growth of the baby.

*Safe temperature, consistency, and formula for offering the baby food.

*What formula and what food should be offered at what stage.

*How to weigh your baby each day and what the weight should be at each stage of development.

*Warning signs the baby is not developing or digesting normally.

There are several sad ways you can lose a baby bird when you don't know what you're doing:

*Crop statis. The food is not being digested or moving properly through the crop.

*Aspiration. Food going down the wrong pipe into the baby's lungs is often fatal to baby birds.

*Burning the crop.

*Feeding too much and causing the baby to regurgitate the food.

*Feeding too little or the wrong formula, causing the baby to suffer from malnutrition or dehydration.

In other words, if your breeder wants you to come in where they can observe you helping out with the baby bird, that's great. If your breeder wants you to take the baby away so they can move on with spending their profits, that is not so great.

# Bird-Proof
# Your Home

If you've owned a pet bird before, you will probably be aware of most of this information. You can use this chapter as a quick checklist to make sure your home will be a safe, welcoming place for your new cockatiel.

If you're a first-time bird owner, you will need to review this chapter with more care. Some hazards in our homes may surprise you, because it isn't obvious that something like a non-stick cooking pan or a potted avocado plant could kill a cockatiel. Take the time to study this information and then to go through your home looking for potential problems before your new bird moves in.

# Throw Out All Your Non-Stick PTFE Cookware

YOUR FIRST STOP IS the kitchen. Polytetrafluoroethylene (PTFE) is the chemical coating placed on non-stick cookware like Teflon to make it easier to clean. If you accidentally overheat or burn an item during cooking, this chemical releases an invisible toxin that overwhelms the sensitive lungs of birds. It works fast. Many victims have reported that every bird in an entire multi-room house or apartment has been killed within twenty minutes.

Some people have also reported mild flu-like symptoms as a result of PTFE poisoning, although humans can be expected to recover their health. Birds rarely survive.

Your cockatiel has a life expectancy of over twenty years. It would be unrealistic to assume nobody in your household ever burns a pan in twenty years. I strongly recommend you to throw away all non-stick cookware coated with Teflon or any other coating that contains PTFE.

The time you save using a non-stick product is simply not worth the risk.

## Consider Your Houseplants

COCKATIELS AREN'T THE chewiest parrots going, but they do explore and chew. Take a walk around the places where your new bird will be spending time— the cage or aviary, the parrot playgym, the places you'll sit with your pet on your knee, arm, or shoulder. Consider each and every plant within the range of a curious beak.

Many popular houseplants are poisonous to pet birds. You will want to sell or give away these plants before your new 'tiel comes home.

***Low-light Lovers***— It is a sad reality that many plants beloved for their ability to grow in dim corners and to thrive on neglect are poisonous. For example, *Dieffenbachia* contains needle-shaped crystals called raphides. Its nickname, Dumb Cane, comes from the fact that humans who chew on it sometimes lose their ability to speak, as well as experiencing a number of other unpleasant symptoms. Adults know better than to chew on the greenery, but both small children and pets have been poisoned by sampling the leaves.

Other popular beauties like *Monstera* and *Philodendron* have also been reported to be harmful to pet cockatiels.

***Avocado*—** Many people enjoy growing small potted trees from the pits of grocery store avocados. Unfortunately, avocado contains a natural fungicide which is deadly to parrots, including cockatiels. Give away your potted avocado to households without parrots.

***Holiday Plants*—** Poinsettia, holly, and mistletoe are all reported to be poisonous to pet birds. Since there are credible artificial options for the holiday season, consider giving away your living poinsettia, holly, and mistletoe to non-bird homes.

There are thousands of species of plants, and you may not be able to find out for sure if any given plant is safe. If you're not sure, make sure your bird is never given access to the plant in question.

Of course, there are many plants that are safe or even healthy for your cockatiel.

*Millet sprouts*— Cockatiels are seed-eaters that often forage on the ground, and they have a special love for seeding grasses. The seeding heads of fresh-grown millet can be a special treat. The main problem with millet is that it can literally grow like a weed if it escapes into your lawn.

*Spider Plant*— This popular, hardy houseplant is beloved for its ability to create "babies" and to keep growing larger and larger with a fairly minimal amount of care. As a bonus, the NASA Clean Air Study proved that they can help absorb common air pollutants found indoors like formaldehyde.

*Boston Fern*— Another safe hardy hanging basket favorite, it is also one of the plants in the NASA Clean Air Study recommended as both non-toxic and capable of absorbing formaldehyde out of polluted indoor environments.

*Chia Pets*— This fun-to-grow houseplant isn't a true cereal or grass. Instead, it's a member of the mint family. Either way, it's both edible and fun to grow. Some people even allow their small pet birds to sample their chia plants on purpose, because they are said to be rich in Omega-3 fatty acid, which is good for your bird's feathers.

# Inspect the New Cage or Aviary

WE'LL TAKE A LONGER look at how to properly house your new cockatiel in the next chapter. For now, it's important to know that you should already have a suitable cage or aviary ready for your new pet.

Are you building the cage yourself? In that case, you should check your materials and complete the construction thirty to ninety days in advance. All parrots, including cockatiels, are susceptible to a form of zinc poisoning called "new wire disease." A form of heavy metal poisoning, this disease occurs when a bird chews new galvanized wire or other new galvanized hardware like nuts and bolts.

New galvanized wire and hardware reacts to the environment by developing a powdery coat of zinc. Therefore, it needs to be weathered for up to three months before it will be safe for the birds to move in. You can speed up the process some by scrubbing down the galvanized hardware with white vinegar, but most people still say you should age this material at least thirty days.

The alternate option, of course, is to construct the new cage from a different material.

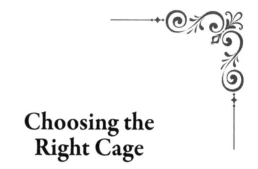

# Choosing the Right Cage

There are many good commercial cages on the market. Alas, there are also many bad ones. It's worth investing the time to make the right choice. A powder-coated metal cage can be an excellent option, as long as it is large enough. Unless it's only used as a sleep cage, you want to provide a minimum area of twenty-four inches wide by eighteen (or even twenty-four) inches deep by twenty-four inches tall. Your cockatiel needs to be able to move around and flap its wings without damaging its long, graceful tail.

Most commercial cages will include a removable metal grate. Since cockatiels are ground feeders, you can use the grate to prevent your pet from dragging its tail through its own droppings.

The cage should be supplied with perches and toys. Be aware that they should be chewable items that you expect to replace on a regular basis. Never punish your 'tiel for destroying a perch or a toy. Chewing is good exercise that helps the bird maintain the health of its beak.

You may have one or two perches made of man-zanita or another long-lasting material, but most of the available perches should be easy-to-chew wood like birch. Avoid perches with those sandpaper surfaces sold to trim the nails. They may or may not work, and they can irritate your pet's feet, causing red sores.

All toys should be rated for cockatiels or even stronger birds like small conures. Some small plastic items labeled as "bird toys" are only intended for budgerigars.

You will also need to buy or build a playgym. Many people start with a portable playgym that they can move from room to room, but they eventually graduate to leaving different gyms set up in all the places where the 'tiel spends a lot of time. Your cockatiel's favorite playground is usually your shoulder or the back of your neck, which means you should also keep on hand a supply of old shirts or smocks you can throw on when you're at home. Cockatiels are not known for their ability to "hold it," so they will tend to leave little gifts on your shirt if you "wear" the bird for a long time.

When choosing accessories for the cage or playgym, you may consider the following items:

*Cuttlebones or Mineral Blocks*— A classic source of calcium. Many cockatiels may ignore it for long periods of time, but make sure you have a clean mineral block available for when your bird feels the urge.

*Mite protectors*— In days gone by, these once-popular pet store items were sold as a cage hanger. You hung it on the cage, and somehow your cockatiel would be magically protected from mites. They don't work, so you can take this item off the to-buy list.

*Millet Holder*— Most cockatiels can't pick up and hold their own food in their foot. If you watch a small conure eat and then watch a cockatiel eat, you will quickly see the difference. You can hold out the branch of millet for your bird yourself, but sometimes you need your hands free to do something else. That's where the millet holder comes in handy.

*Cockatiel Toys*— Buy toys from reputable suppliers that are specifically designed for cockatiels. Your bird will be chewing and scrambling on these items, so you want them to be safe. Some people offer their cockatiels those little plastic mirrors. I do not. Cockatiels can be among those whose birds who believe a reflection in a mirror is a potential rival or lover. As a result, the mirror can spark aggressive or possessive behaviors.

*Travel Cage or Carrier*— A small travel cage gives you a convenient way to transport your cockatiel to the vet, bird sitter, or groomer, as well as an easy way to move your bird to a new home, to a vacation destination, or during an evacuation for a natural emergency like a hurricane.

A word of caution: Don't uses the travel cage ON-LY for visits to the vet or groomer. Put treats in there from time to time. Use it as another playpen. Otherwise, your cockatiel will form a negative association with the travel cage and give you more of an argument when you bring it out.

Most new bird owners plan to spend most of their time with their pet cockatiel indoors. However, here are some issues to consider if you're thinking about building a large aviary outdoors for a flock.

# Protection from Predators Large and Small

ALL BIRDS ARE EDIBLE. A small parrot like a cockatiel can attract a surprising number of potential enemies, including rodents, snakes, cats, raccoons, and even birds of prey like hawks or owls. The most deadly enemy of all is often the mosquito that carries diseases like avian pox or West Nile Virus.

A good aviary must offer protection from all of these predators, both large and small. You will want to use two layers of screen— an inner layer of strong hardware cloth capable of keeping out the bigger predator and an outer layer of pet-proof non-chewable mosquito netting.

## Protection from the Elements

ONE OF THE GREAT ADVANTAGES of an out-door aviary is that your birds can enjoy natural sun-light, which helps their bodies make vitamin D3. Without this vitamin, your cockatiels can't properly use calcium, the mineral which helps build strong bones and eggshells. In their wild environment, cock-atiels would have access to all the natural sunlight they need, but they are often deprived of this invisible source of vitamins in our homes.

However, this isn't a license for you to expose your cockatiels to extremes of heat or direct sunlight. Your birds must always have access to shade and a place where they can cool off out of the sun.

Cockatiels are also fairly tolerant of cooler temperatures, as long as they have been properly acclimated. Make sure they have a dry, warm roost box, and a winter flight or cage where they can be protected from frost.

# Protection from Losing Your Birds

COCKATIELS ARE NOT usually considered expensive birds who would attract the attention of a thief, but you still need basic security to protect your flock against people who act on impulse.

*A good privacy fence may keep people from seeing or accessing the aviary.

*Good locks should be installed on the gate and the aviary.

*Web cams or baby monitors can be an inexpensive way to keep track of who is coming and going.

*Walk-in aviaries should have a double door (air-lock-style) system. Both doors should never be open at the same time.

# Mixed-Species Aviaries

COCKATIELS ARE SOMETIMES chosen for a home walk-in aviary because they are gentle toward smaller birds. It isn't unusual to be able to keep finches and perhaps a pair of small doves or button quail in the same aviary. However, you need to inform yourself about all of the species you plan to place together. Some small birds are highly aggressive.

For example, you shouldn't house cockatiels and lovebirds together. The lovebirds might be smaller, but they are aggressive and will almost certainly push the 'tiels around. They could even corner your 'tiel and inflict a severe injury.

Before setting up your own aviary, you should consider joining a local bird club or networking in another way with local bird-keepers. People who are already successfully running a mixed-species aviary will be your best source of advice.

Make sure there are more roost boxes than pairs of birds. Don't skimp on perches, toys, treats, or food and water dishes either.

And, of course, you should be sure that your mixed-species aviary is, in fact, a genuine aviary with plenty of room for all birds inside to go about their own business. Cockatiels should never be asked to share a standard cockatiel cage with a member of another species. Smaller, stronger birds like lovebirds have actually removed toes from their cockatiel companions.

# Bringing the
# New Baby
# Home

The big day has finally arrived. Your baby cockatiel is weaned and ready to come home.

You should already have the cage, playpen, and other supplies ready and waiting for your new cockatiel. We'll talk about everything you need in a later chapter to make sure you haven't missed out on anything. For now, let's focus on how to welcome your new pet into your household.

Everybody will be excited, but make an effort not to overwhelm the 'tiel with too many people and too many noises all at once. A hand-fed baby 'tiel isn't afraid of their humans, but anybody can become overwhelmed in a new situation. Speak in calm, relaxed tones. Keep the ambient noise low by playing soft music rather than loud games or violent television programs. Really, just use some common sense.

Hand-fed 'tiels are used to being the center of attention. It probably won't be long before they're seeking attention. If you sense that your baby is interested and relaxed, you are ready to move your new 'tiel out of the cage or carrier.

Never grab a cockatiel. They may associate the feeling of being grabbed with the sensation of being captured by a predator. Since 'tiels hold grudges, one careless grab could destroy your baby's trust.

Your breeder has probably already demonstrated the "Step up" command to you. Some 'tiels learn to step on a perch that is inserted into the cages. Others prefer to step on a hand or a balled-up fist.

My personal preference is to never stick a hand into a parrot cage. Instead, I insert a perch and hold it against the 'tiel's chest while saying, "Step up." The 'tiel can ride the perch out into the open, where I can then offer the hand, arm, shoulder, or playpen.

Cockatiels have a short attention span. Don't plan on a two-hour bonding session. Instead, plan multiple five to twenty minute bonding sessions over the course of a day. Short, enjoyable encounters are much better than long, tiring sessions. Since hand-fed babies don't fear humans, a grumpy baby can nip or bite. You always want to end the session on a positive note before it ever gets to that point.

Hand-fed cockatiels may bob their heads when they're hungry. They may also sit in a perfectly good food bowl that has more than enough food, if only for the sense of security they remember from being in the brooder. Don't worry. It's normal.

# Bringing Home the Rescue or Older Cockatiel

Some readers know they are going to bring home an older cockatiel. This chapter is for them. Some of these birds will present different challenges, but they can also present different rewards. There are a number of reasons to adopt an older cockatiel, so let's quickly hit the high points.

*You prefer to provide a home to a 'tiel who needs rescue. You can make a difference for a bird who might otherwise have trouble finding a home. Although they can be one of the most easy-going feathered pets around, cockatiels can end up in rescues, often for one of two reasons.

*They are powerful flyers.* A lost cockatiel might go for hundreds of miles away from where it started. In the past, this author has rescued cockatiels who were brought down by storms. They were fully flighted and could have come from anywhere, since they weren't chipped or banded. I tried, but I was never able to locate their original owners. In those cases, I had no choice but to allow somebody else to adopt the birds.

*They have a long life expectancy for their size.* I own a rescue cockatiel in his twenties because his original owner passed away. Sometimes, people experience other life changes which mean they can no longer provide their pet with a good home.

*You already know the bird or the person who must surrender the 'tiel, and you know you are compatible. In that case, you are in a situation to learn as much as you can about the bird's history and its particular health and personality challenges. For instance, I was asked to rescue an older 'tiel who was being pushed around by the younger birds in his aviary. With this information, I was able to provide him with his own cage where he could see, talk, and interact with my other birds, but not be pushed around. Later, I was able to teach him how to share a playgym.

Since he can meet his social needs in a neutral shared place and still retreat to the security of his own territory, his personality has truly blossomed. He has become a happy, active pet.

As a bonus, he surprised me by whistling a number of tunes he must have learned from a previous owner. His talent was silenced as long as he was being pushed around. Once he had his confidence back, he could start to sing again.

*As it happens, some people prefer to adopt a 'tiel already trained to talk or whistle. Such birds aren't always easy to find, but they do save you from the tedious process of teaching the 'tiel to whistle yourself. Also, not every cockatiel can learn to whistle, so it can be a good idea to adopt a bird who is already trained if the bird's talent is extremely important to you.

*You have found a 'tiel and have been unable to locate the original owner. As your relationship grows, you decide to keep the bird.

Any of these reasons are perfectly fine reasons to open your home to an older cockatiel.

## Getting Off On the Right Foot

START BY GETTING A health exam, especially if you have other birds in the home. Protecting the pets you already have should always be your priority.

In an ideal world, you would always adopt your older 'tiel during a relatively calm, stress-free period of your life, when you can devote plenty of time and attention to your new bird. Life doesn't always work out that way. A sudden death or a disaster like a fire could leave you with a homeless bird who needs help today, whether or not your own situation is entirely ideal. All you can do is all you can do. Fortunately, cockatiels are resilient birds. Their big issue is being isolated. You don't want to take in one of these highly social birds, only to stash it alone in a dark corner for long hours of the day.

Keep the bird with you as much as you can, even if you can't take it out of the carrier. Seeing you and talking to you means a lot to a cockatiel.

In some cases, an older cockatiel may be skittish in a new situation. Don't panic. These domestic-bred birds have almost certainly been handled at some point, so they can learn to enjoy being handled again if you're patient.

For instance, someone brought me an adult cockatiel in his late teens who was said to be frightened of hands. This bird was obviously tame and already knew how to step up on a perch or an arm on command. He knew what "step up" and "come" meant. He was simply afraid to follow through if you presented him with a bare hand.

I didn't have access to the 'tiel's entire past history, but cockatiels do hold grudges, and I have to assume somebody in his past used to grab him with their hands. Therefore, teaching this bird to step onto a hand became a matter of slowly developing the bird's trust. At first, I did nothing more complicated than putting a hand somewhere on the playgym where the 'tiel was playing. Later, I began to offer millet spray treats in my fingers. Like many 'tiels, he is unable to hold his own food, so if he wanted to eat the millet, he had to approach my hand.

Every day for a few minutes at a time, I practiced the "step up" technique of asking the bird to step onto my arm or perch. He already knew how to do this, but I wanted him to get comfortable with doing it over and over again with me. Each individual sessions was short, often as short as five minutes. Nothing good would come of stressing an older 'tiel who might have a tendency to form grudges. Calm, loving patience is the key.

He loved attention and loved the game of moving from arm to arm. After a time, instead of offering my arm, I moved him into my balled-up fist.

He didn't even notice he had just stepped onto the much-hated hand.

Now, this bird still doesn't go to my hand one hundred percent of the time every time I ask. Sometimes, I do have to offer the arm instead. But we're getting there.

What if you discover that you have an older bird who has never been handled by humans or taught to step up? This is actually pretty rare, since pet cockatiels in most countries outside Australia itself are going to be domestic rather than wild birds. They have been bred for generations, and the basic techniques are well understood. Most breeders understand the importance of training baby birds to "step up" on command.

Still, it is always possible to encounter an aviary bird that was never tamed as a pet because the 'tiel was kept as part of a breeding pair or aviary colony. In that case, you may have a real challenge.

The first step is to get someone else to clip the wings. The rescue may have already done that for you. If not, ask them to start the bird with a fresh wing clip and nail trim. Remember, cockatiels can hold grudges, so you don't want to start off on the wrong foot.

Give your new 'tiel some time to settle into your home in a safe, quiet place where the bird can observe you and your family. Allow the bird to have its own cage on its own territory. They have a natural desire to socialize and interact, but if they have never experienced that with a human, they may take a lot longer to come around than your average 'tiel.

Talk to your new bird in a quiet, patient voice. Don't grab at the cage or stick your hand in the cage. Your goal is to slowly encourage the bird to come to you. After a few days, when it's obvious the 'tiel is calm when you approach, you can try something like holding a millet spray through the cage bars to coax the bird forward.

You are building trust.

The next move is to open the cage door and offer a perch at the height of the 'tiel's breast while giving the "Step up" command. Don't badger the bird. Make the offer for a few minutes at a time. Parrots, including 'tiels, have a natural urge to step up on a branch presented at just the right height. Once the bird catches on, you can start (slowly) allowing the bird to ride a little way on the stick.

Try to end every session on a positive note. Tell your 'tiel, "Good bird. Smart bird." It might seem silly, but they do understand.

Keep offering the millet spray or another favorite treat on a daily basis.

As your 'tiel develops confidence, you will be able to offer the stick, get the bird to step up, and ride out into the open, where you can teach your new pet to step onto a playpen, your arm, or your shoulder.

Again, patience is the key. Never grab a cockatiel with your hands, because they associate being grabbed with being hunted by a predator. You could lose all that carefully built-up trust in a moment.

If you must pick up your 'tiel because they are in a dangerous situation— perhaps, they startled and flew to the ground where they are underfoot— use a towel to pick them up. They won't be thrilled, but it's better for them to hold a grudge against a towel than against you.

# What To Feed A Cockatiel

Cockatiels are relatively easy to feed because they evolved to eat seed. However, a wild 'tiel undoubtedly forages far and wide over the course of a lifetime, eating not just dry seed but fresh seeding grasses, sprouts, and perhaps even a protein-rich insect or two. Cockatiels might not need as extensive and expensive a diet as many parrots, but they won't live up to their potential if they are kept strictly on a diet of dry seed and water.

Australian bird-keepers often recommend a seed-based diet. Make sure the diet is a high-quality seed formula designed specifically for cockatiels, who prefer smaller seeds like millet and canary seed. You should also offer access to finely chopped vegetables that includes such items as turnip tops, collard greens, mustard greens, kale, Swiss chard, dandelion greens, chickweed, fresh or frozen sweet corn, grated carrot, grated zucchini, broccoli florets, snow peas, spinach, and bell pepper. Clean, fungus-free sprouts, including sprouting millet, are often a well-accepted treat.

It can be a struggle to get a cockatiel to recognize chopped salad as food. As a result, many people have developed various birdie bread or cockatiel bread recipes to tempt their pets into eating a more varied diet. You can bake a loaf if you have several birds, but if you have only one or two cockatiels, you should probably make muffins. In that way, you can freeze some of the muffins for a future date.

There are many recipes available online. Here are a couple to get you started.

# Sweet Potato Cockatiel Bread

SWEET POTATO, YAM, grated carrot, or pumpkin are all valuable vegetables for helping our cockatiels consume enough beta carotene, which converts to vitamin A in your bird's body. Although sweet potato recipes are widely available for humans, you need to cut way back on the sugar and spices when adapting them for your cockatiel. The powdered egg shell is a valuable source of calcium.

### Ingredients

1-3/4 cup all-purpose flour

1 tablespoon baking powder

1 tablespoon brown sugar

½ cup finely chopped walnuts

½ cup finely chopped raisins, dried cranberries, dates, or figs

2 large clean eggs including the shell

¾ cup unsweetened apple juice

1 cup cooked mashed yams, sweet potatoes, carrots, or pumpkin

¼ cup canola oil

Preheat the oven to 425 degrees Fahrenheit. Grease the muffin tin or loaf pan. Stir together the dry ingredients. Crack the eggs, and carefully crush the shells as fine as you can with a wooden cooking mallet. Add the powdered shell to the other dry ingredients. Scramble the eggs with a fork, and then mix together with the apple juice, mashed vegetable, and oil. Blend into the dry ingredients.

You can now spoon the bread batter into the loaf or muffin pan. Cooking time depends on your oven, as well as the size of your muffins or loaves, but I would set the timer for 25 minutes and keep checking every five or ten minutes after that. The bread is done when you can stick a knife in the center, and it comes away clean, without any sticky batter on it.

Let cool, then remove the bread from the pan. Individual muffins can be kept in the freezer for a couple of weeks and defrosted the same day you want to serve them to your birds.

# Jiffy Corn Muffin Miracle Birdie Bread

COCKATIELS ARE PICKY birds. Some people may quibble about using a commercial corn muffin mix, but this bread sometimes tempts a bird who might otherwise resolutely refuse to eat vegetables.

### Ingredients
2 boxes of Jiffy Corn Muffin Mix (the standard 8.5 ounce size)

2 large eggs

1 can yellow cream corn

1 can whole kernel corn, drained

Preheat the oven to 350 degrees Fahrenheit. Grease the muffin or loaf pan. Break the eggs, and use a wooden food mallet to grind the shell into powder. (Skip this step if people will be eating the bread along with the bird.) Scramble the raw egg with a fork. Stir both cans of corn into the egg. Stir in the Jiffy Mix.

For some reason, you can never get all the lumps out of cornbread batter. Just mix it up well enough, and don't worry if lumps remain. Pour into the loaf or muffin pan.

As before, set your timer to make the first check at 25 minutes if you were baking muffins. You can go to 45 minutes without checking if you're making a whole loaf. After that, keep checking back every five or ten minutes, depending on the progress.

The bread is done when you can stick a knife in the middle and bring it out clean.

Some people who offer a seed-based diet may choose to supply a good cockatiel pellet as ten percent of the diet instead of offering the birdie bread. A lot depends on how much time you like to devote to food preparation, as well as to close observation of what foods your bird actually eats.

# An Alternative Diet

SOME COCKATIEL OWNERS, especially in North America, are fans of the modern pelleted diet. A stubborn cockatiel who picks out only its favorite seeds can

be at risk of a nutritional deficiency. Avian vets and nu-
tritionists have worked to develop a pellet which supplies balanced nutrition in every bite.

If your hand-fed baby cockatiel was brought up on
pellets, you have a fairly easy job. Simply continue to
offer the recommending pellets as the core of the diet. Chopped vegetables, birdie bread, cockatiel honey
sticks, and millet sprays can be offered on the side as a
special treat.

What if your cockatiel was brought up on seed?
Should you switch to pellets? You will get good people
arguing on both sides of this question. Since 'tiels are
picky eaters, they may present you with quite a battle if
you try to get them to switch away from their favorite
and familiar food. Some birds may refuse to accept pellets as food.

Don't try to convert your new pet to pellets from
the very first day you bring the 'tiel home. The bird
needs time to adjust. Later, if you decide your cockatiel
isn't eating a good, balanced diet with seeds at the core
of the diet, you can talk to your avian vet or a more ex-

perienced cockatiel keeper who can offer you suggestions about how to make the transition.

Converting a cockatiel from seed to pellets can be a long, drawn-out process. You might begin by offering pellets alone for an hour or two in the morning. Later, mix in some of the pellets with the seed bowl. It can take an amazingly long time for a cockatiel to accept a pellet as food. Some people try offering the seed for an hour in the morning and another hour in the evening, while leaving the pellets available at all times.

However, you don't want to risk starving the 'tiel. Buy a small kitchen gram scale, and make a note of your bird's weight each day. This is not a weight-loss diet. A starving bird is not healthier than a bird who eats nothing but seed.

Some cockatiels will never recognize pellets as food. Don't panic, or make feeding time into a battle of wills. There are other techniques for getting your 'tiel to eat a better diet. One way is to sprout millet sprays and other small, clean seed. The green sprouts are still recognized as food, but the sprouting process has increased the nutritional value of the seed.

Keep in mind that many popular parrots like conures are from moist, rich, tropical climates where they would eat a variety of fruits and vegetables, not just seeding grasses. Cockatiels, budgerigars, and lovebirds come from a climate that is dryer and much less lush. They can be more conservative and less adventurous when it comes to their food, and that's perfectly natural.

# Supplements

AS A GENERAL RULE, cockatiels who eat a pellet-based diet get enough vitamins and minerals from the pellets. Cockatiels who prefer a seed-based diet should have a good avian vitamin and mineral supplement powder that can be sprinkled on soft food they're willing to eat, such as berries or greens. There are medical situations that may require you to offer special supplements such as calcium, but you should give these supplements on the advice of a vet who has examined your bird.

# What Not to Feed a Cockatiel

*AVOCADO AND GUACAMOLE.** As we mentioned in the section on houseplants, avocado contains a natural fungicide called persin. The fungicide is most concentrated in the pit, leaves, bark, and skin, but it may also appear in the edible fruit. Since persin is poisonous to parrots as well as to fungus, you should never share this food with your cockatiel or include it in the birdie chopped salad.

*Caffeine and theobromine.** Both of these stimulants can be hazardous to a bird's heart. Caffeine is found in coffee, green and black teas, and some colas. Don't allow a curious 'tiel to have a sip of your drinks. Theobromine is found in chocolate. Dark chocolate is the most dangerous to birds, but you shouldn't share any of our chocolate goodies with a 'tiel.

*Alcohol.** No pet bird should be sampling our adult beverages, because they become intoxicated and lose their balance after only a tiny taste.

**Uncooked meat, fish, seafood, or poultry.** The picky cockatiel is unlikely to go after these foods, but pet birds do love to investigate our kitchens. Always wipe off carefully after preparing raw food.

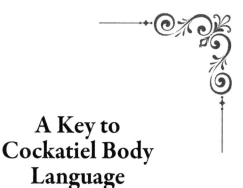

# A Key to Cockatiel Body Language

If you have owned birds before, a lot of this information will be familiar. However, cockatiels are a popular choice for a first bird. You may be great at reading people or even at reading dogs, but some avian behaviors may seem hard to understand at first. Never fear. With a little experience, you will soon be reading your 'tiel's body language like a champ.

**\*The bird is grinding its beak at night.**

This is a tricky one. People who grind their teeth are probably under significant stress, so we assume a 'tiel grinding its beak is also under stress. Actually, the opposite is true. The 'tiel is relaxed and getting ready to fall asleep.

**\*The bird is backing into a corner with its beak open. It may even be hissing.**

This one is just what it looks like. The 'tiel is angry, upset, and wants to be left alone. You are at risk of being bitten if you insist on pushing yourself on the bird at this moment.

**\*The bird is lifting a foot up in a defensive posture like it is trying to push you away.**

This is another defensive posture. Again, you're at risk of being bitten if you push yourself on the bird right then. Let your pet calm down.

**\*The bird is hanging upside-down and flapping its wings.**

While this vampire bat game can look aggressive, it usually means the 'tiel is just playing and getting some exercise.

**\*Tapping or slamming/throwing/dropping items for attention.**

The tapping sound is a cute way cockatiels (especially males) may use to attract the attention of a potential mate. In some cases, the bird may use it to attract you. In other cases, I have seen the tapping sound used to draw out a friend in another cage. One of my birds uses the tap against the bottom of his cage to attract his favorite playmate if he thinks it has been too long since they've been allowed to play together on their shared gym.

Once you've heard the tap, you won't confuse it with the slam. Hitting toys or pushing items off tabletops can be a way to demonstrate aggression or work off anger. Some 'tiels are better left alone when they're in a grumpy moods. Others— especially the ones who are sliding things off your tables or countertops down to the floor— are probably trying to get your attention. They may need a little more one-on-one time.

**\*Bird is sitting puffed-up fat and possibly on the ground or floor.**

This 'tiel is feeling sick and should be taken to a vet as soon as humanly possible.

**\*Bird puts its head low and pushed in your direction.**

This 'tiel wants you to scratch its head. Work carefully, especially if you feel any plastic-like sheaths on new feathers. Removing too much of the sheath at once can stop feeling good and start feeling painful. Be very attentive to your bird's responses. Closed eyes, and head remaining lowered, is a sign that you should continue.

**\*Male bird holds his wings away from his body and thrusts out his chest.**

People refer to this as the "heart," and some people say it's a demonstration of the bird's machismo or excitement. He's letting you know he's the man. The intent is often to impress you with how important he is.

If you're watching your 'tiel from behind during this posturing, you can see the so-called heart shape created by the open wings.

**\*The language of the crest**

All cockatoos, including the cockatiel, know how to use their head-feathers to communicate emotion.

The little differences in the position of the crest may seem confusing at first, but soon you'll be reading your 'tiel like an open book.

The relaxed, happy 'tiel usually displays a visible but relaxed crest that is curled back in a jaunty manner.

If the crest is lowered so that it's totally flat, uh oh. Is the bird also hissing, by any chance? This 'tiel is angry and feeling aggressive. You need to let this bird calm down, because this 'tiel is in no mood to play around.

A frightened 'tiel can lift its crest all the way up tall in a posture of obvious tension. They may also tense up their bodies to look tall and tense to match. Something may have startled the 'tiel, even something as minor as a noise from outside. Look around to find the source of the fear. Offer calm reassurance. A soft voice could go a long way here.

# Should Your Trim Your Cockatiel's Wings?

I always recommend that pet bird owners keep their cockatiel's wings trimmed, even if they don't trim the wings of any other bird in their home. I am not sure if anyone keeps official statistics, but I hear from a surprising number of people every year who have lost their cockatiel. The problem arises because cockatiels are fast, strong flyers who become easily confused once they're away from the guidance of their flock.

They evolved to fly hundreds of miles in a desert climate. How far can they fly in a rich climate where they can drop in here or there to grab snacks from a bird feeder? An escaped cockatiel might eventually come down again, but your pet could be so far away that the two of you never find each other again.

In addition, most populated areas of the world present significant hazards to an escaped pet bird that likes to feed on the ground. Cats, dogs, rats, snakes, hawks, owls... the list goes on endlessly. One of the rescue cockatiels brought to me had been soaked through in a torrential downpour and found in the middle of the street. It was only a matter of good luck that the bird (otherwise healthy) wasn't run over by a car.

A secondary reason for clipping the wings is to avoid injury in the home. Because they are such powerful flyers, if they are startled and hit a wall, a mirror, or a ceiling fan, they could experience a significant injury.

Finally, since they do enjoy walking and scrambling, as well as flying, cockatiels have other ways to exercise. In fact, clipping the wings may give them more opportunities to exercise, since you are more likely to take them out on their parrot playgym if you aren't concerned about them taking off and bonking their heads.

However, read me carefully here. I recommend you get the cockatiel's wings clipped. I do NOT usually recommend that you perform the wing-clipping yourself. Many people report that cockatiels hold grudges. Therefore, it's a good idea to have a vet or bird groomer take care of the job for you. That way, even if your bird does hold a grudge, it won't be against you or anybody in your home. The professional wing clip usually ends up looking a little neater than the home cut too.

**Important to know: A wing clip is not permanent surgery. You are not really clipping the wings. You are clipping the fully grown-out primary feathers. You never cut into living, growing blood feathers. Therefore, a properly performed clip doesn't hurt the bird any more than a properly performed haircut hurts you.**

However, just as hair grows back, feathers grow back too. Keep an eye on the molt. Sooner or later, you will need to return to the groomer for another trim, or else your cockatiel will be fully flighted once again. Several people have told me their cockatiels were lost because they didn't realize the feathers had mostly grown back.

# If you decide to keep a flighted cockatiel

IF YOU DO DECIDE TO allow your cockatiel's wings to grow out, you face some special challenges. You will need to take exceptional care to make sure your bird doesn't get lost in the wild. Develop strong habits. When you're home and have your bird out, make sure the doors and windows are secured from the inside. If someone walks in unexpectedly, your curious 'tiel could be halfway across town before you know it.

A big problem is that cockatiels love to cuddle up and go to sleep on your neck or shoulder. When they're snoozing quietly away, it's oh-so-easy to forget they're even there. If you walk outside with a bird on your shoulder, one bark from a neighbor's dog could startle your pet away and send it flying away.

Make a habit of checking your shoulder and your bird's cage every time before you open the door to the outside world. Every. Single. Time.

Some people have trained their cockatiels to accept a flight harness, which means they can take their bird outside without being at risk for losing their pet. The key to using a flight harness is getting the bird to accept wearing the harness in the first place. If you have a hand-fed baby who was handled from an early age, and you have continued to handle the bird with confidence, you may be able to slowly introduce your 'tiel to the idea.

Leave it out for a few days near the cage or play-gym, so the bird can see the harness is perfectly harmless. Eventually, you can move forward with putting it on the bird.

Cockatiels who are fearful of being grabbed or toweled are less likely to ever accept the harness. Your 'tiel must be tolerant or even enjoy being handled. You have the greatest chance of success if your bird has learned to allow you to lift under the wings, to pat lightly on the back, and to rub the head and neck without reacting with a hiss.

# Bathing and
# Grooming the
# Cockatiel

In the wild, flocks of cockatiels will fly a long way to be near water. Many of these birds love to bathe, and they should be given every opportunity to do so. Pet cockatiels are individuals, and different birds love to bathe different ways.

Many cockatiels will enjoy being presented with a shallow dish that holds about an inch of lukewarm water. For some reason, shallow water can really invite the birds to splash around.

There are special perches you can install in your shower stall if you're one of those people who enjoys showering with your cockatiel. Make sure your pet is only splashed with clean water that isn't too hot, too cold, or too strong. Don't get soap, body wash, or shampoo on your bird.

I like to mist cockatiels twice a week in the morning. Most of the time, you will be spraying pure water from a room temperature mister than has never contained anything except pure water. Use a light touch. Some cockatiels have long memories. If you blast a bird too hard just once, that bird may fear the mister forever.

Sometimes, instead of pure water, you can mist with one of those bird feather formulas designed to make your cockatiel glow. They seem to work fine, especially if they contain aloe, but they are not mandatory by any means.

A well-groomed cockatiel must also have neatly trimmed nails. In the wild, the bird would be exposed to a lot of different perches and bark textures in a lot of different situations, and apparently there are many more opportunities for the nails to get worn down without the help of your friendly neighborhood groomer. Unfortunately, in captivity, even with the best of care, it's unrealistic to think you can get by without regular nail trims.

Of course, you should make every effort to promote good foot health. Your bird should have a variety of perches in different sizes, styles, and widths, so your cockatiel isn't always sitting the same way and putting pressure on the same spot. You should also provide a variety of toys. However, most cockatiels don't or can't lift items with their foot, so there are a very limited number of things you can do. At some point, you will have to either visit the groomer or trim the nails yourself.

Taking your 'tiel to the groomer is probably the best idea for most people. If you do have a grudge holder, your bird can hold the grudge against somebody else, which is always preferable to having the bird hold the grudge against you.

However, if you have a cockatiel that is relaxed about being handled all over or even wrapped in a towel, then you may find it just as easy to do the job with the help of a friend or family member. Get all your equipment together before you start, including an old clean towel, the nail clippers or nail file, and the styptic powder. Everybody involved needs to be calm and relaxed, because trimming the nails never goes faster if you try to hurry. This author likes to approach the grooming like a game.

One key is to have some of the towel draped over the bird's head to conceal its view of the room. Cockatiels, like most parrots, are programmed to relax in the dark. Sometimes, the bird will settle in to chew on the towel. Great. Now is the time to carefully take hold of each toe in turn to clip off the very end. Don't cut too deep. It's better to have to repeat the exercise next week than it is to cut into a blood vessel and startle your 'tiel.

Accidents do happen. Don't get upset or excited if you do hit a blood vessel. Continue to talk calmly, in a low, reassuring voice, as you apply the styptic powder to the bleeding toe under pressure. The blood should clot in a minute or two. You want to avoid making a big deal over the accident, because you want the cockatiel to forget the whole thing ever happened. The 'tiel will pick up on your energy. If you remain calm, the bird usually returns to a relaxed state almost immediately.

# Taming and Training Your Cockatiel

Taming and training a cockatiel can be very, very easy, or it can be very, very hard, but it always requires at least some investment in time. Cockatiels are flock animals. All parrots are social, but 'tiels in particular can become unpleasantly needy and demanding if they feel neglected. They may shriek, tear out their own feathers, become overly aggressive, or even lose their wonderful pet quality.

The bottom line:

Don't adopt a cockatiel at time when life is going crazy. The time to adopt is when you will have a lot of free time available to spend with your new pet. Even the sweetest, most accepting hand-fed baby 'tiel needs your time and presence to develop into the pet the bird was intended to be.

This is not to guilt you if something happens, and life changes. If something happens that interferes with your ability to spend quality *and* quantity time with your cockatiel, you have options like introducing your bird to a second bird who can be a full-time companion. However, your dream cockatiel is a bird who loves to be with you. This dream can only come true if you have time to make it come true.

For many people, the brand new baby cockatiel will seem like a deceptively easy pet. The bird comes already tame, thanks to the work of the hand-feeder. The bird already wants to bond with somebody, thanks to its own strong social instincts. All you have to do is show up and let the magic happen. What could possibly go wrong?

Well. Yes and no. Cockatiels aren't hard to work with, and a hand-fed baby should be a real treat. Nonetheless, you can't expect any shortcuts to forming a strong bond between you, the new bird, and your family. Believe it or not, you have to put in the time, even with a supposedly "easy" bird like the 'tiel.

Pet cockatiels sometimes seem to do better with people who are retired or who work out of home offices. The hand-fed baby came to them already tame, and these owners have the time to invest in *keeping* the bird tame.

Your cockatiel wants to be an important part of your life. As we mentioned earlier, you can set up a play area in each room where you spend a lot of time with the bird, or you can use a portable playgym. You should also devote time each day to allowing your bird to play on your arm or shoulder. Your cockatiel may seem to be doing nothing more important than snoozing or nuzzling at your hair, but these simple pleasures mean the world to these birds. Put in the time with your birds, and your sweet baby will stay tame well into old age.

One good way to engage your cockatiel is to teach little tricks. There is one trick this author believes every pet parrot should know and practice— the Step Up command.

A pet cockatiel that steps onto a hand, arm, fist, or perch on command will be infinitely easier to move around with you in the course of a day. For example, say your cockatiel has flown to a high perch like a curtain rod. You can offer the stick while saying, "Step up," and a well-trained bird will climb onto the stick. Then you can move the bird where you want it, such as a playgym.

If you're starting with a hand-fed, domestic-bred cockatiel, you shouldn't have much trouble teaching this basic command. In some cases, the seller may have already taught the command.

If not, you have a little work to do.

*Start by getting your new bird used to being around you. Make sure the bird knows that you are now the person who is offering treats like millet or sunflower.

*The basic concept is simple: You are going to build on a parrot's natural instinct to move to the highest available perch. You can start the training with your arm or with a stick, but this author usually begins by using a stick just because it's easy to manipulate. Hold the stick at the 'tiel's breast level while giving the command. The 'tiel may or may not understand the command, but sooner or later the bird is going to climb onto the stick.

*Any time the bird succeeds in stepping up, you offer a small treat while praising the bird. The attention may be as important as the treat to the cockatiel. These birds are motivated by attention.

*Over time, the bird learns to associate the words, "Step Up," with the action of stepping up onto the perch. The bird will also associate these words and actions with positive attention. Soon, a habit will form. You offer the stick and say, "Step Up," the bird will step up automatically.

*Eventually, you won't need to pay off with a treat. You will simply say, "Step Up," and your bird will be happy to do it.

*You should also practice moving your cockatiel from perch to perch. Otherwise, an adoring cockatiel could be difficult to peel off your shirt when it isn't in the mood to move away from you.

*This author likes to practice by playing a sort of ladder game with the new cockatiel. Hold the perch at your bird's breast level, and say, "Step On." Then offer a new perch at breast level. And so on. Don't be annoying. Do it a few times a few minutes at a time. Keep the mood light and fun.

A note:

Be cautious about adopting an untamed single cockatiel. Older aviary-bred cockatiels are resistant to change, and sometimes can't really be tamed, only trained to perform a trick in response to a clicker. Good animal trainers can train adult 'tiels— after all, they can even train tigers— but an amateur may have trouble transforming an older aviary cockatiel into a pet. These birds may never view you as a part of their flock. To provide them with a satisfying social life, you should be prepared to offer a feathered friend.

# Talking and Whistling

Your cockatiel is probably not going to be the next talking parrot sensation. They tend to have squeaky, unclear voices that are difficult to understand. That said, some people do train their cockatiels to speak, and some unusual birds (especially males) have a surprisingly large vocabulary for a small parrot.

In the wild, male birds most often vocalize to impress female birds and to claim territory. As a result, most people who want to teach their cockatiels to talk prefer to work with male birds. Some females do learn to talk though. Either way, you need to start with a young bird and to bring along a boat-load of patience.

Higher-pitched human female voices seem to capture the attention of any parrot better than deeper or lower-pitched male voices. Cockatiels are no exception. If possible, pitch your voice higher during the training sessions.

Each session should take place in an otherwise quiet room, perhaps with the cockatiel on your hand, so that your pet can focus on what you're saying. Repeat the phrase for no more than ten to twenty minutes a session. Remember, birds have very short attention spans. You can offer more than one session a day and probably should. However, don't sit down for a solid hour and try to get a lesson in all in one chewy chunk. Your cockatiel will simply learn to tune you out.

More cockatiels learn to whistle tunes than learn to speak phrases. If your patience is at a premium, you may want to skip the talking lessons, and stick with teaching whistled tunes. It isn't necessary for you to be able to whistle, although your bird might pay more attention in the beginning if you do. It's perfectly fine to use a recording.

Again, set a timer. Play the tune for ten to twenty minutes a session. You want your pet to find the tune interesting enough to copy. A bored bird will respond by ignoring or shrieking at the annoyance.

# Cockatiel Mutations

One of the reasons cockatiels seem special is because they look special. They are the only commonly kept pet parrot that has a long graceful tail to counterbalance a tall, expressive crest. Check out the cockatiel's big brothers, the cockatoos, and you will see what I mean. Their tails are much shorter in proportion to their wings and body.

As a result, the cockatiel has an elegant profile that stands out from the crowd. The bird looks stylish, especially because its natural colors are gray and white accented with bright pops of yellow and orange. What fashion designer could have done better?

The natural wild color of cockatiels is called Normal Grey. Virtually every wild cockatiel (with very rare exceptions) is a Normal Grey bird. They give an overall impression of being gray birds with a large white wing stripe. Adult males feature bright yellow faces that set off the famous orange cheek spots. Adult females and all younger birds have much duller faces, although the orange cheek spots are still visible.

Adult females and immatures also have light but noticeable yellow barring on their tail feathers, a fact that becomes important later.

Despite being easy to breed, the cockatiel got off to a slow start when it came to the development of the various color mutations. Various texts disagree about which mutation first caught the eye of breeders, with some authorities saying it was an albino and others saying it was a pied. However, most sources seem to agree the first serious cockatiel mutation breeders got started in the United States in the mid-twentieth century. At some point in the 1950s, the Lutino mutation emerged in Florida, and the cockatiel breeders suddenly had a hit on their hands.

Lutinos lack the gray in their plumage. Thus, they appear in shades of white to bright yellow. These cheerful birds can be truly beautiful, since the yellow tones in their face as well as the bright orange cheek spots remain. However, there's a catch with this mutation. Because the gray is completely removed, you can't assume that a bird with a bright yellow face to set off the bright orange cheek spot is a guaranteed male. It can just as well be a female because the gray that would otherwise be there to mask her face doesn't express itself.

You can check for the yellow barring on the tail, but even this is not guaranteed, since some adult males also retain the barring.

If it's important to be certain of the sex of your Lutino, you should opt for DNA testing.

Another problem with Lutinos is that this particular mutation is also associated with a mutation for baldness. Many Lutinos have a bald spot behind the crest. Although this bald spot doesn't hurt your pet in any way, you may feel frustrated if you selected your pet on the basis of its looks. Always check with a vet if your 'tiel suddenly develops a problem with its feathers, but the Lutino bald patch is not an illness or an injury but a natural genetic variation.

Many breeders work to eliminate the baldness gene from their stock. Ask around for a local reference.

Lutinos have bright red eyes because of the lack of dark pigment.

A related mutation, the Albino, is a pure white bird that lacks the yellow and orange pigment as well as the gray. Its plumage is all white, its eyes are red, and its feet are pink. (Some experts object to the word Albino being used for this mutation, but many people do use it because it's more efficient than calling it something like a White-faced Lutino.)

One of the earliest mutations was the Pied, which describes a bird that has irregular patchworks of light and dark plumage. No two Pied cockatiels look exactly the same, and you can't tell the sex of the Pied 'tiel by looking at its face or tail feathers. This is another mutation where you'll want to do DNA testing if it matters to you what sex you have.

The Cinnamon mutation is similar to the Normal Grey, except that the gray is touched with a hint of brown. Adult males tend to be browner than adult females, and adult females will also have the barring on the underside of their tails.

A related mutation is Fallow, which can be described as a Cinnamon with red eyes.

In recent decades, the White-faced or White Face mutation has exploded in popularity. In this handsome bird, all yellow and orange pigment has been replaced by white. While some people might wonder how removing the pop of color could be an improvement, there is no doubt that White-faced cockatiels are truly stunning birds when seen live in the flesh. The tall crest, the graceful tail, and the formal coloring of gray and white somehow come together to create a specimen who wouldn't look out of place at Paris Fashion Week.

The adult males with their pure white faces are especially striking. Females and immatures have more gray on the face.

An interesting note is that a breeder will recognize a baby White Face from the moment it hatches out with pure white fuzz instead of yellow or yellowish fuzz.

Another popular mutation is the Pearl. The "pearl" comes from the fact that each affected feather has a spot of white or yellow on it, which creates the effect of a bird covered with speckles or spots. Adult females keep their beautiful pearls for life, but adult males usually lose most or all of their spots as they mature. When you pick out your hand-fed baby, ask about the gender if you want to be sure the bird keeps her pearls for life.

All in all, at the time of writing, there are twenty-two recognized cockatiel mutations. On top of that, mutations can be combined. Because the pearls are so attractive, many birds may have the pearl mutation combined with something else. For just one example, a cinnamon cockatiel might have pearl markings.

Since the possibilities are endless, you have lots of options for choosing a unique cockatiel. However, some colors can never appear, like blue, because this species lacks the necessary pigment.

Even the so-called Emerald or Olive mutation isn't especially green, unless you have a really good imagination. In this mutation, the main body color is a pale gray washed with yellow that some people evidently can see as olive. Well, maybe. If you ever have the pleasure of seeing one of these rarities, you can make up your own mind about that.

The complex genetics behind these mutations is beyond the scope of this book. If you are interested in this topic, you are strongly advised to join a respected cockatiel organization, where you can network with experienced breeders who can point you to multiple resources where you can study the science behind the development of these beauties.

However, if you're curious about color mutations, there are three terms you'll hear over and over again, so they are well worth knowing. This author is offering the nickel tour, not a course in genetics, so take these simplified definitions as a starting point. You'll need a much bigger, more in-depth volume if you want to delve deeply into the science of cockatiel mutations.

(And you can feel free to skip over the next few paragraphs if this material is too technical for you. Not everyone will want or need this information.)

**\*Dominant—** A dominant trait will be expressed. You don't have to wonder if the bird is carrying a hidden gene for the trait. A good example is the Dominant Silver mutation. Just like it sounds, these 'tiels are a light silver color. (Double Factor Dominant Silvers are a lighter shade of silver than Single Factor Dominant Silvers.) They also happen to have DARK eyes and can be easily sexed in the same way Normal Grey 'tiels are sexed, by the brightness of the male's face and the barring on the female's tail.

It's an over-simplification for many genes, but for color mutations, you can assume that a bird gets a gene from each parent for any given trait. If the bird gets a dominant trait from one parent and a recessive trait from the other, the dominant trait will be the one that is expressed.

**\*Recessive**— A recessive trait can therefore be hidden. It will only be expressed if the bird gets a copy of the gene for the recessive trait from *both* parents. In cockatiels, a good example is the Recessive Silver mutation. This is a silver cockatiel with RED eyes.

Many cockatiels are so-called splits. This means they have a dominant trait and a hidden (recessive) one. If you happen to breed two birds who have the same hidden trait, and they both pass the hidden trait to one of their youngsters, you can have a baby who grows up looking very different from either of the parents.

No shenanigans necessary. Mama cockatiel didn't sneak out and get busy with a different male while you weren't looking. It's just science.

**\*Sex-Linked**— These traits are a little more tricky for most of us to understand. With sex-linked traits, the female gets only one gene from her father. Since she gets only the one sex-linked gene, that is the trait she expresses. *She can't be split to a sex-linked trait because the gene can't be masked by a more dominant trait.*

However, the male receives a gene from both parents as usual. The dominant gene will express itself if it's there. *Therefore, he can be split with a hidden recessive gene in his DNA.*

You might be wondering if that's right. Yes, cockatiel genetics is a little bit like Opposites Day compared to human genetics. Human males have only one X chromosome. In cockatiels, females only have the one chromosome. So, if all of this sounds backward to you, now you know why.

Many popular mutations are sex-linked, including the Lutino, the Cinnamon, and the Pearl.

Why is this important?

*Females get only one gene for any given sex-linked mutation, a gene donated by their father.* However, the males get a gene from each parent. He would need to get the same sex-linked recessive gene from both of his parents to express that gene. Therefore, it's possible for a male bird to carry a hidden gene for a sex-linked trait that he can pass down to his own youngsters even though he doesn't express the trait himself.

You can make predictions about a pair's offspring based on what mutations the parents express.

For example, we know that the Lutino mutation is sex-linked in cockatiels.

If both parents are Lutino, you will not be surprised to learn that all of the offspring will also be Lutino.

However, if the male is a Lutino, and the female is a normal Grey, the male offspring will all look like normal Greys but will carry a hidden gene for the Lutino mutation. By contrast, all female offspring will be Lutino.

This means, in this situation, you can visually sex your baby birds from an early age.

If the female parent is the Lutino, and the male is the Normal Grey, all of your babies will look like Normal Greys. None of the female offspring will carry the Lutino gene. However, the trait is not lost. All of the males will carry the gene and have the potential to pass it on to a future generation.

If you're confused, relax. There is no reason to get too deep in the weeds. Cockatiel genetics is an absorbing and rewarding hobby that supports serious breeders and exhibitors. Join and support your local cockatiel organization to meet experts and exhibitors who can lead you deeper into this fascinating world.

In the United States, you may want to join the National Cockatiel Society. In Australia, you may consider the Australian National Cockatiel Society. Whatever group or club you join, there is no better way to learn the intricacies of cockatiel breeding and exhibition than by allowing yourself to be guided by the experts.

# Common Cockatiel Problems

Cockatiels are relatively easy to care for, especially if you are realistic with yourself about how much time they actually demand. However, they are living beings with personality quirks, and sometimes owners do meet with some challenges.

Here are some issues you might face and how to deal with them. However, please remember that no book can be a substitute for medical care. If your cockatiel has a medical emergency, contact a veterinarian as soon as possible.

# Help! My Cockatiel Bites!

COCKATIELS AREN'T BIG birds, and they're known for their sweet personalities, so it's always a shock when you realize your adorable little 'tiel is capable of biting hard enough to draw blood. Hard-fed birds don't know their own size, but they do have their own opinions, and they can be capable of getting into the bad habit of biting to get their way.

A bad habit is always easiest to break before it has formed.

Therefore, you need to learn your cockatiel's body language. Cockatiels are prey animals by nature. They don't want to fight or to bite or to engage in conflict. They'd like to head off a problem before it ever starts. Therefore, they almost always warn.

Look for these warning signs, and give your bird time and space to chill out if your bird offers the following threats:

*Hissing— Cockatiels can hiss like a snake if they're annoyed. While hissing, they may often lay the crest down flat against the head.

*Pinning eyes— Many parrots, including cockatiels, can dilate and contract the pupils of their eyes to express anger. It sounds subtle, but once you know what it looks like, it's an obvious sign of fury.

*Trying to look bigger— A threat is always more impressive from a larger, more imposing animal. An angry cockatiel may fan the tail, lift the wings away from the body, or puff out big to send a message that this bird is a serious threat.

*Lunging— At this point, the 'tiel is no longer simply issuing a threat. This bird will try to bite if you keep pushing it.

Some common situations can inspire a threat or even a bite.

*Territorial issues— Like most social birds, cockatiels have a natural instinct to claim some small bit of territory as their own. In the case of pet 'tiels, that territory is almost always their cage. That's their safe place, and most birds are happiest if your hand is never placed in or on the cage. Teach your pet from an early age to step onto a stick, and use that stick when moving your 'tiel in and out of the cage.

*Hormones— Sometimes, even solo birds act out because of misplaced breeding hormones. I never offer a mirror to a 'tiel or a budgie, because they may fall in love with their own image and then become frustrated when the image never reciprocates. Grouchy, frustrated 'tiels may bite. You can also frustrate them through inappropriate petting on the back or vent

*An Older Bird Who Wasn't Properly Socialized— Cockatiels are flock birds who need to be socialized from an early age. If you have an older bird who wasn't properly socialized, it can be difficult or impossible to teach it to accept being handled by humans. Review the information about bringing home a rescue bird, and develop patience. You might also consider the possibility that this particular 'tiel may do better as an aviary bird than a shoulder pet.

# Stop the Screaming

COCKATIELS CAN'T TOLERATE long hours alone. They were evolved to be members of large, wide-ranging nomadic flocks. A wild cockatiel might never be alone in its life. Even though today's pet 'tiels are domesticated birds, the reality is that they still have the same social instinct. If they can't see their flock members, they will call out to make contact.

If they don't get a satisfactory response, they may call persistently, and their loud, repetitious screams are not all that pleasant. They are small, and their lungs are not ever going to compete with a jet engine, but they are related to the cockatoos after all, and they'll certainly give it the good old college try if they feel they have to.

Here is one way the problem begins:

A lonely bird may start screaming for attention. Even if the attention your pet receives is negative, it's still attention. A drama is created, and the bird temporarily forgets its own fears of being separated from its flock. Thus, the drama becomes its own reward. Bird screams, you run in and scream at the bird to be quiet, bird figures out that you react every time it screams so it screams more to keep in contact with you... and so it goes, around and around, in a vicious spiral.

When you first bring your new 'tiel home, you want to start by introducing your pet slowly to its new environment. You may choose a quiet place where the bird can study its new home at its own pace. However, if the quiet place is a little too quiet and isolated, the 'tiel may panic because it feels isolated and isn't sure what happened to its brooder buddies.

You may have to tinker a little to find the ideal spot where the bird can see you and get to know you without feeling overwhelmed by its new environment. You can try placing a partial cover on the cage so your bird can see you but also retreat at will. This "new bird nerves" should settle down in a few days as your 'tiel gets used to watching you come and go.

However, sometimes the screaming surprises you later in your relationship. This can happen when you get busy and start spending less time with your pet. The reason could even be a good one (longer hours at a new job, new baby, or so on), but all the 'tiel knows is that it's suddenly spending long hours alone.

This, to a cockatiel, is intolerable. Hence the screaming.

Fortunately, the problem is not that hard to fix. This author has encountered whiny, anxious cockatiels who called repeatedly every time they were left alone. These 'tiels were moved into new situations where they never had to be alone, and the screaming soon stopped.

For example, I was recently asked to rescue a cockatiel in his late teens. This 'tiel turned out to be an extremely anxious and dependent bird who cried even when I went no farther out of sight than the next room. Fortunately, the screaming habit wasn't long established. It may have started after a former owner passed away. In any case, it was clear that this bird was highly stressed whenever he was left alone, even for only a moment or two.

Changing the bird's fundamental psychology probably wasn't going to happen, especially not at his advanced age. Instead, I took away the bird's need to scream by making sure he always had a flock member close to hand. How? Simple. The bird was moved into a home with a multi-bird owner who worked out of her house. The 'tiel could spend hours every day in contact with its human. And, when the humans weren't home, the cockatiel was placed in a spot in the bird room where he could see and talk to several other small parrots in nearby cages.

With its social need for constant contact being met, this cockatiel stopped screaming.

# Night Frights

NIGHT FRIGHT IS A COMMON condition in cockatiels. Most parrots probably have poor night vision, but cockatiels in particular are effectively blind in the dark. Therefore, they can panic if they hear something that frightens them. The same panic instinct is triggered if they see a very brief flash of light that disorients them, like a lightning bolt or the headlights of a passing car in a window.

In the case of the cockatiel, they appear to have an instinct to take off and fly immediately. Of course, since they are in their sleep cage, this attempted flight causes them to hit the ceiling or to thrash around. In their panic, they can seriously injure themselves. Many 'tiel owners have reported that they woke up in the morning to find blood in the cage as a result of their bird thrashing around so violently they broke a blood feather.

If the cockatiel is already bleeding, you need to act fast to clot the wound. As first aid, apply styptic powder or clean white flour to the wound under pressure. And get to your avian vet as soon as possible.

However, as always, preventing problems is better than fixing problems.

Most people recommend keeping a night light on in the bird room, as well as a corner of the cage cover lifted so your bird can actually see the light. You should have a source of white noise in the room to blur out noises from outside. A small fan or even a phone app that creates the white noise is fine.

Finally, if you hear your cockatiel thrashing anyway, check it out. The bird could be responding to an actual threat, such as a mouse in the house.

To avoid startling a sleeping bird, always talk or sing in a low voice when you enter your 'tiel's room at night.

The goal is to provide up to twelve hours a night of peaceful, uninterrupted sleep in a secure place.

## She Won't Stop Laying Eggs

INCESSANT EGG-LAYING is a common and life-threatening problem that can arise with female cockatiels.

Any adult female bird in season can lay eggs even if she doesn't have a mate. Of course, these eggs will be infertile, so you need not worry about what do with any potential young. The real issue is that calcium— the same mineral that builds strong bones— is required to build strong eggshells. Therefore, if your 'tiel lays too many eggs, her body can be depleted of this vital mineral, in turn causing multiple serious health problems, including egg binding.

As the name suggests, egg binding occurs when the egg gets stuck in your bird's cloaca. If not treated promptly, this condition results in the death of the bird.

Lack of calcium can also result in weak bones that break easily, another life-threatening medical emergency.

Obviously, the best way to prevent these problems is to discourage your cockatiel from laying eggs. Since egg-laying is sparked by hormonal changes in her body, we have to figure out a way to encourage her body to stop producing eggs.

One trick is to remove the real eggs and to replace them with dummy eggs. Let her sit on the fake eggs for a few weeks until the urge to lay fades away for another season. Most people place one fake egg in the nest for every real one they take away, but you can sometimes trick her into ending the laying process sooner by placing two fake eggs in the nest for every real one you take away.

Why does this work?

In the wild, when predators remove eggs, the female will try to lay again if the conditions are still right to raise a family. Similarly, if she breaks a weak clear egg, she'll lay again to replace that. Her body is triggered by its desire to create a nest that contains the "right" number of eggs.

As a result, if you keep removing the infertile eggs and leaving her with an empty nest, she'll probably keep laying. Some pet cockatiels end up trapped in a cycle of laying eggs over and over again, until her body is completely depleted of nutrients.

However, once her body believes she is already sitting on the "right" number of eggs, the hormones usually shift, turning off the desire to lay and moving forward with the desire to sit on the brood. After a couple of weeks or so, she will get bored with the project when the eggs fail to hatch.

In addition to supplying fake eggs, you can make some other adjustments in the bird room to tell her body that it's a bad time to nest. For example, you need to control the amount of light she's exposed to, since long hours of light are associated with spring and summer weather. Make sure she has a dark, comfortable, quiet place where she can sleep undisturbed for twelve hours a night.

Some people find it helpful to remove any roost boxes that resemble natural cavities where cockatiels would nest. If they feed a lot of soft, cooked food, they may also need to switch to dryer fare for a time.

However, other people have noted that their cockatiels simply laid the eggs in her food dish if she didn't have a box, so your mileage may definitely vary.

An important takeaway: Any cockatiel who keeps laying eggs day after day after day is at risk of sudden death, especially from egg binding. Consult with your avian vet as soon as possible. Hormone shots are one possible treatment that could save your bird's life.

When should you be concerned? A single clutch of eggs is not a problem. Wild cockatiels are evolved to lay one or two clutches a year if the conditions are right to allow them to raise their offspring. A domestic cockatiel may lay an egg every couple of days until she has completed a clutch of up to eight eggs.

If she keeps on laying after that, you should definitely check in with a vet.

# Breeding Cockatiels At Home

B reeding cockatiels, especially for exhibition or to develop new mutations, can be a rewarding hobby. In many parts of the world, especially North America, Europe, and Australia, you should find it relatively easy to meet active breeders through your local bird club or cockatiel society. This author never advises anyone to go it alone when they're trying to learn how to breed healthy birds. The guidance of more advanced cockatiel breeders will help you avoid needless mistakes.

Think about why you want to breed cockatiels before you set up the first nest box.

Good reasons to breed cockatiels:

*You want to hand-feed and train your own babies from the very beginning.

*You want to develop new color mutations.

*You want to develop a strong, healthy line of 'tiels who will win prizes at exhibitions.

A bad reason to breed cockatiels:

*You need some extra cash, and you want to raise baby birds to sell.

This author strongly advises you to never breed any bird if you are short on space or money. Since cockatiels are domesticated pets who seem relatively easy to work with, you may think they are an exception to this rule. They're not. Setting up the breeding cages or aviaries can cost you more money than you stand to make— especially since cockatiels sell for relatively low prices.

Another issue is the time and cost of housing and placing the baby birds you raise. Even if you have a good-sized property, don't run ahead of yourself and breed too many. Every baby hatched must be fed (preferably hand-fed), socialized, and housed. Is there really a demand for any more cockatiels in your area?

In some areas, there are too many cockatiels already housed in rescues. If you can't sell your baby cockatiels, do you have the space to house them and the time to care for them?

In this author's opinion, breeding cockatiels as a hobby can be rewarding— but breeding them as a profitable business can be brutal. If you want to breed 'tiels for profit, get hands-on, real-life information. Network with your local club, local experts, and local vets. This book is for hobbyists and pet owners, so we won't talk more in this volume about how to breed cockatiels as a business.

## The Breeding Cage or Flight

YOU MUST FIRST DECIDE whether to breed your cockatiels in cages or in a large colony. If you are planning to breed certain color mutations or to pair certain birds, the choice is made for you. You will need to breed in cages, with each pair given its own secure cage where it can rule the roost on its own territory.

However, it is certainly possible to set up a large pen or colony that allows the members of your flock to select their own mates. You lose control of who chooses to pair with who, but you have fewer cages to set up and clean, and you may find this option more relaxing, although you are unlikely to breed any prize-winning show birds this way.

Important to know: Most birds can't count very high, but if the colony is too small, it is possible for them to keep track of a potentially deadly "pecking order."

In other words, you should have either a single pair per enclosure, or you should have "many." A so-called colony that contains three, four, five, or even six birds could be a recipe for disaster. The top pair in such a small group can remember who the bottom bird is, and they can literally harass the lowest-ranked individual to death. Then the group will form a new social order, with a new bird on the bottom who will be harried and harassed in its turn.

You see the problem.

Many, if not most, hobby breeders will find it far more practical to place each pair in its own cage or flight.

# Setting up the Perfect Nest Box

COCKATIELS, LIKE MOST parrots, are cavity nesters who can't build their own nest. If you started with lovebirds, you may have seen them collecting material and building nests just like many of your garden birds do in your trees and shrubs. Cockatiels can't do this. They have to find, not build, their nest cavity. And, since both parents attend the nest, it will need to be roomy enough to accommodate both adult birds at once as well as growing babies.

That means if you want to breed a pair of cockatiels, it will be your responsibility to provide them with a suitable nest cavity. Fortunately, that is very easy, since they are eager to accept a basic wooden nest box of the right size. Many pet stores, feed stores, and on-line pet suppliers can offer you a choice of suitable cockatiel boxes.

I strongly recommend you to select a box that allows you to attach the nest to the outside of the cage or flight. The box should have an access door or window that opens outward. In that way, you can easily check on the progress of the nest without sticking your hands in the cage or the nest box itself.

This author will not recommend any particular brand of commercial nest box because I prefer to build my own. If you have a few tools in your workshop or garage, you can easily do the same.

A typical cockatiel box is at least ten inches high and wide to accommodate the adult bird's long crests and tails. The entrance hole can be a long rectangle or even a circle three inches wide or more. That isn't too important. Entrance holes to cavities in rotten trees vary in size too. Just make sure the entrance is both wide enough and smooth enough not to injure your birds as they go in and out.

Since cockatiels are not nest builders, they are not going to do much to fancy up the interior of the box. Here is a little trick some breeders use to make the eggs a little more comfortable and not so roly-poly. Cut out a flat piece of wood that will fit just inside the box to become the floor. Use a hole drill to cut a three inch diameter circle out of the center of the flat. Sand down around the hole you made to make sure there aren't any pointy, scratchy places that could catch on a bird.

Now, when you put the floor on the bottom of the nest box, you have a nice concavity where your female cockatiel can lay her eggs and not have them roll around all over the place.

Not everybody does that, and you do not have to, but I believe it is well worth doing if you can.

What about material to line the nest? Again, your cockatiels will not add their own. It is your responsibility to soften the bottom of the nest with safe nontoxic material. While it is true nobody is putting nest material in a wild tree cavity, we can presume that old rotten cavities found in the wild are soft by nature.

In any event, many people line the floor with a couple of inches of wood chips or shredded paper. You can also buy clean, non-toxic nesting material from the usual places where you buy pet bird supplies.

And this author does realize not everybody adds the nest material, especially if they do provide a nice concavity for the eggs. Observe your birds, and do what works for your birds.

# A Quick Note About Hand-feeding

MOST HOBBY BREEDERS want to hand-feed the birds they breed. Hand-fed babies can make superior pets because they have grown up from an early age accepting humans as a source of food. However, if you think back to the chapter on choosing a baby cockatiel, you'll remember that we talked about why an inexperienced bird owner should never take home an unweaned bird.

Hand-feeding requires a deft touch. You won't pick up the proper technique from reading a book, and therefore we won't try to fill out pages with a blow-by-blow description of something best learned in person. This author strongly advises you to find a way to learn under the watchful eyes of a more experienced hand-feeder. An older friend who is willing to supervise the first few times you hand-feed can be worth their weight in gold.

That said, many people also find it helpful to study some of the cockatiel hand-feeding videos you find on YouTube or elsewhere on the internet. These videos have the advantage that you can slow them down and watch them over and over to gain confidence in your understanding of how you should approach the task.

However, even a video is no serious substitute for someone who is willing to give you a hands-on education. Join your local club. Volunteer at your local rescue. Do what it takes to develop your skills and reputation as someone who is willing to put in the work to learn how to do the right thing for their birds.

♫♫

*If you enjoyed this book, please return to the retailer where you bought it to leave your review. A five-star review is a great encouragement to a new author.*

*Still not sure a cockatiel is right for you? Consider the lovebird, the subject of my new book, **Your Dream Pet Lovebird: Twenty-first Century Care, Feeding, Training, and Breeding Strategies.***

# About the Author

Darla Birde is the owner of a small bird rescue that does not re-sell the birds in her care. She has worked with lovebirds, cockatiels, budgerigars, and many other birds for over a decade.

Made in the USA
Las Vegas, NV
15 September 2022

55339626R00076